Contents

How to use this book

Do you know how to write a convincing advert, a thrilling recount or clear instructions?

This book will show you lots of different kinds of non-fiction writing.

HOUSE FOR SALE

What do you think of this advert? Does it make the house sound its best? How could it be improved?

> **FOR SALE**
> **295 Newtown Way**
> A great house in a terrible area. Any offers?

Perhaps this advert will sell the house. It emphasizes good points and ignores bad ones. It appeals to as many people as possible.

Below is a list of good and bad points about the house.

Good points	Bad points
• Very big.	• Noisy aeroplanes.
• Smart gates.	• Traffic fumes.
• Safe, neat garden.	• Graffiti.
• View of hills.	• Nearby pylon.
• Shops nearby.	• Smells from the dump.
• Lots of space.	• Could be rats!
• Good security.	• Needs more security.

Here are some people who might like this house.

Pilot (close to airport)

Keen gardener (big garden)

Large family (lots of space and a garden)

Supermarket worker (could walk to work)

Lorry driver (close to major road)

A really boastful start.

Gardeners and families will like this.

There's no need to say how close!

People like bargains.

FOR SALE
295 Newtown Way

Magnificent family house with charming walled garden and splendid iron gates.
Walking distance from local shops, roads and transport. Handy for airport. Interesting views.
Burglar alarm, automatic security gates and entry phone.

Bargain price – £95,000

This can mean lots of bedrooms.

Sounds very grand.

This might interest pilots or business people.

This makes the house sound safe.

There are two double pages for each style of writing. The first one (see the example above) shows you how to plan your writing and gives you a model of a finished letter, advert, recount or chart.

Sometimes there are labels to help you, or a table like the one on the right.

Good points	Bad points
• Very big.	• Noisy aeroplanes.
• Smart gates.	• Traffic fumes.
• Safe, neat garden.	• Graffiti.
• View of hills.	• Nearby pylon.
• Shops nearby.	• Smells from the dump.
• Lots of space.	• Could be rats!
• Good security.	• Needs more security.

The second double page (see the example below) gives you step-by-step instructions to create your own piece of writing.

Read the instructions carefully before you start writing.

Writing an advert

Write a tempting advert for one of these two places.

1. First make a list of good and bad points about it.
2. Think who might like to live there and why.
3. Write FOR SALE at the top of your advert.
4. Write the address.
5. Describe the house and garden. Keep it short.
6. Give buyers an idea of what is nearby – shops, transport and landmarks.
7. Describe the view and any special features.
8. Say how much it costs.

WRITING TIPS

When you write an advert:

• use enthusiastic adjectives:

splendid	impressive	amazing
glorious	delightful	fabulous
stunning	luxurious	magnificent

• use appealing adjectives to cover up any faults:

cosy = tiny
interesting = strange
private = in the middle of nowhere
popular = expensive
extraordinary = you won't believe your eyes!

Rewrite this using all you have learned about writing adverts.

FOR SALE

Flat 236, Terror Towers

Filthy, tiny flat with crumbling balcony on 13th floor. Deafening noise from dogs' home and local amusement arcade. Trains almost pass through kitchen. Surrounded by huge building site. Decorated throughout in black and red.

Overpriced at £30,000

8   9

WRITING TIPS

The writing tips explain the particular rules for each style of writing.

The pictures are full of extra ideas to make your writing come alive.

Sometimes there is a box of useful verbs or adjectives.

Enthusiastic adjectives:

splendid	impressive	amazing
glorious	delightful	fabulous
stunning	luxurious	magnificent

You can either use these suggestions or think of other suitable words.

HOUSE FOR SALE

What do you think of this advert?
Does it make the house sound its best?
How could it be improved?

SUPERMARKET

FOR SALE

Below is a list of good and
bad points about the house.

Good points	Bad points
• Very big.	• Noisy aeroplanes.
• Smart gates.	• Traffic fumes.
• Safe, neat garden.	• Graffiti.
• View of hills.	• Nearby pylon.
• Shops nearby.	• Smells from the dump.
• Lots of space.	• Could be rats!
• Good security.	• Needs more security.

Here are some people
who might like this house.

Pilot (close to airport)

Keen gardener (big garden)

Large family (lots of space and a garden)

Supermarket worker (could walk to work)

Lorry driver (close to major road)

Perhaps this advert will sell the house. It emphasizes good points and ignores bad ones. It appeals to as many people as possible.

A really boastful start.

Gardeners and families will like this.

There's no need to say how close!

People like bargains.

This can mean lots of bedrooms.

Sounds very grand.

This might interest pilots or business people.

This makes the house sound safe.

FOR SALE
295 Newtown Way

Magnificent family house
with charming walled garden
and splendid iron gates.
Walking distance from local shops,
roads and transport. Handy for airport.
Interesting views.
Burglar alarm, automatic security
gates and entry phone.

Bargain price – £95,000

Writing an advert

Write a tempting advert
for one of these two places.

1. First make a list of good
   and bad points about it.

2. Think who might like
   to live there and why.

3. Write FOR SALE at the
   top of your advert.

4. Write the address.

5. Describe the house and
   garden. Keep it short.

6. Give buyers an idea of
   what is nearby – shops,
   transport and landmarks.

7. Describe the view and
   any special features.

8. Say how much it costs.

WRITING TIPS

When you write an advert:

- use enthusiastic adjectives:

splendid	impressive	amazing
glorious	delightful	fabulous
stunning	luxurious	magnificent

- use appealing adjectives to cover up any faults:

cosy = tiny

interesting = strange

private = in the middle of nowhere

popular = expensive

extraordinary = you won't believe your eyes!

Rewrite this using all you have learned about writing adverts.

FOR SALE

Flat 236, Terror Towers

Filthy, tiny flat with crumbling balcony on 13th floor. Deafening noise from dogs' home and local amusement arcade. Trains almost pass through kitchen. Surrounded by huge building site. Decorated throughout in black and red.

Overpriced at £30,000

PACKING UP

Mrs Jones is moving house. She has
many precious possessions to pack.
This calls for some clear instructions.

Imagine wrapping this valuable po
Think about what you would do
and in what order.

Here is one way to pack the pot safely.
You may have thought of a different way.
It doesn't matter as long as the pot is safe.

How to pack a pot

You will need:

- newspaper
- bubble wrap
- strong tape
- strong cardboard box
- polystyrene chips
- marker pen

What you do:

1   Remove the lid and make sure the pot is empty.

2   Stuff the pot with screwed-up newspaper.

3   Wrap the pot first with newspaper, then with bubble wrap.

4   Use strong tape to keep the wrapping in place.

5   Wrap the lid in newspaper and tape it to the top of the pot.

6   Screw up some newspaper and put a layer in the cardboard box.

7   Put the pot carefully in the box.

8   Fill the box with polystyrene chips and bubble wrap.

9   Close the box with strong tape.

10 Label the box **FRAGILE**.

Writing instructions

Write clear instructions for packing one of these items.

A huge glass tank full of fierce fish

Lots of frozen food

1. First think how you would wrap the object.

2. Write the title: **How to pack a...**

3. Write the heading: **You will need**

4. List the materials you need. Write them in the order that you will use them.

5. Write the heading: **What you do**

6. Write exactly what to do, step by step.

A set of delicate china

A fancy glass chandelier

WRITING TIPS

When you write instructions:

- write in the present tense.
- only describe one activity at a time.
- number each instruction.
- begin each instruction with a verb.
- start each instruction on a new line.

Use bossy verbs (imperatives) to explain exactly what to do.

place	use	protect	roll
label	fill	wrap	unscrew
stick	take	cover	remove
stuff	pack	empty	screw

POINTS OF VIEW

What do you think about doing homework? Do your parents think the same? Does your teacher agree?

What do your friends think? The best way to find out everyone's opinion about homework is to ask them.

I'm tired after school so I can't concentrate on homework.

Me

Homework keeps you out of mischief!

Granny

I try to help you but I just muddle you – I don't know how things are taught at your school.

Mum

Doing homework helps you learn to organize yourself and remember what to bring home.

Dad

When you have homework you don't have time to play with me.

Little brother

It's good for you to work alone, so I can see what you understand.

Teacher

I can't go to Sports Club because of all my homework.

Best friend

You can put people's opinions on a 'For' and 'Against' chart like this.

the
nent
top.

this
top
left-
column.

each
reason
a
point.

with
ment
what
hink
vhy.

Write this at the top of the right-hand column.

Children should do homework.	
For	Against
• Children practise what they learn at school. • Children learn more. • Children learn how to organize themselves. • Children are kept busy. • Children are more confident because they have learned things well.	• Children are very tired and can't do their best. • Parents may muddle children by explaining things wrongly. • Children don't have time for playing or their hobbies.
I think that children should do homework because it helps them learn.	

For and against

Choose one of the statements on these pages. Think of reasons for and against it. The pictures give you some ideas.

1 ★ First do some research. You might:
- interview people you know.
- write to people.
- make a questionnaire.

2 ★ Next make a chart. Put the statement at the top. Divide the page in half. Write 'For' in one column and 'Against' in the other.

3 ★ Write as many reasons as you can in each column.

4 ★ End with a conclusion saying what you think and why.

All children should be given pocket money.

Children should play sport every day.

WRITING TIPS

When you write your chart:

- start each opinion with a bullet point.
- when you write an opinion, try to think of the opposite view too.
- give a reason for your final decision: 'I think that... because...'

ALL ABOUT ANIMALS

Reports are factual. They explain the way things are. This information about penguins is from an animal handbook.

BIRDS Emperor Penguin

HABITAT

Emperor Penguins live in seas around Antarctica, in large groups called flocks.

APPEARANCE

The Emperor Penguin is the largest of all penguins.
Height: 1.15m
Weight: 30 kg

Small bill

Oily, waterproof feathers

Thick blubber keeps penguin warm

Wings used for swimming not flying

Small feet

Tail steers when bird is swimming

BREEDING

In the autumn, male and female penguins travel 100 km south to a nesting site. There, they meet a life-long mate. Three weeks later, the female lays one egg. She returns north to feed, leaving the male to care for the egg.

The male keeps the egg warm on his feet under a flap of skin. He does this for two months. He eats nothing and huddles together with other males to keep warm. When the egg hatches, the female returns to feed the chick. The male can feed at last.

FEEDING

Penguins are fast swimmers (up to 30 km per hour). They catch fish, squid and krill in their beaks which they eat under the water.

This report is based on the information and pictures found in the handbook.

Emperor Penguins

Emperor penguins have black heads, wings and feet and white tummies. Their necks are bright yellow. They are the biggest of all the penguins.

They live in Antarctica, which is a very cold place. They have waterproof feathers to keep dry and fat to keep warm.

Penguins have wings but they cannot fly, though they swim fast. They use their wings like flippers and steer with their tails. They catch their food while they are swimming.

Wings push along

Tail steers

Krill

Squid

In the autumn, penguins travel to nesting sites. The female penguin lays one white egg. The male puts it on top of his feet to keep it warm. The female goes away to eat. The male penguins stand close together to keep warm. They do not eat for two months. The female returns when the egg hatches and then the male can eat. Baby penguins are called chicks.

egg

egg cracks

chick

I saw some chicks at the zoo. They had soft, fluffy, grey feathers instead of black and white ones. The mother was feeding them with fish straight from her mouth into theirs.

Most people love penguins and we need to protect them.

look

e
live

What
they do

What
they eat

Their
babies

ter's own
ments

A good
ending

19

Writing a report

Write a report about giant pandas
or African elephants.

MAMMALS Giant Panda

HABITAT

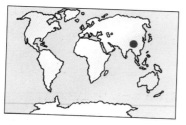

Pandas live alone in the
cold, high bamboo forests
in the mountains of China.

BREEDING

Female pandas produce
one or two babies (cubs)
every two or three years.
Cubs weigh only about
100g and have no fur.
Cubs need a lot
of care and usually
only one survives.

APPEARANCE

Height: 1.7m
Weight: Up to 150 kg

Eyes have good
night vision

Powerful jaws

Thick fur

Hairy feet
for walking on
snow and ice

FEEDING

Pandas live mostly on
bamboo shoots and roots.
Sometimes they eat small
animals, birds and fish.
Adult pandas eat up to
38 kg of bamboo each day.

Large paws
for grabbing
shoots
and roots

Sharp claws

1 First read the information.
Look up any words you do not
understand in a dictionary.

2 Make a list of the following
questions and jot down the
answers as you find them.

- What does the animal look like?
- Where does it live?
- What does it eat?
- What do you know about
  its babies?

MAMMALS African Elephant

HABITAT

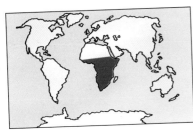

Elephants live in large groups called herds on the grassy plains of Africa.

APPEARANCE

Height: 3.7m
Weight: Up to
   7 tonnes

BREEDING

Females (cows) give birth to one baby (calf) every four or five years. The calves weigh 90 kg and are 1 metre tall. They drink their mother's milk until they are six years old.

FEEDING

Elephants spend up to 18 hours a day grazing on grasses, leaves, roots, tree bark and fruit. An adult can eat up to 230 kg of food and drink 200 litres of water every day.

Large ears flap to cool elephant

Thick skin

Tail swishes flies away

Long trunk for smelling, sucking up water and picking up things

Tusks for digging and fighting

3 The neat copy. Write the title.

4 Write your report using the answers to your questions.

5 Add facts of your own. Look in other books to make sure they are correct.

WRITING TIPS

When you write a report:
- write in the present tense.
- start a new paragraph for every answer.
- end with a short conclusion.

WHERE AM I?

Imagine you have just arrived at the station of this town. You are going to meet a friend at the cinema.

Your friend has given you some directions and a map. Read the directions and trace your route on the map.

Station Road

STATION

Bridge Street

High Street

River Way

CAFÉ

Turn right out of the station and walk straight along to the end of Station Road.

Turn right into the High Street and go as far as the second set of traffic lights.

Turn left into Bridge Street.

Take the third turning on the right into Upper Street. The cinema is halfway along the street on the left.

Writing directions

Now write directions
from the cinema to
the café by the river.
Use these steps to help you.

1 Find the cinema and the café.
Trace the route between them
with your finger.

Pretend you are starting
with your back to the
cinema – then you won't
muddle your rights and lefts!

2 Write directions using bossy
verbs (imperatives) such as:

turn	take
cross	go straight along
follow	walk

3 Every time the route changes
direction, write a new
instruction on a new line.

WRITING TIPS

When you write directions:

- always use street names
  where possible.

- mention useful landmarks
  such as a police station,
  a garage, a hospital,
  a park or a school.

MY AMAZING NEWS

Everyone loves to talk about something exciting that has happened to them.

These pictures show the main events of a family's adventure in the snow. Can you recount what happened?

2

3

4

First look at the pictures. What is the setting and who are the people? What happens first, next and later? How does the adventure end?

Here is one way of writing
an imaginative recount
of the events.

Adventure in the snow

Last Sunday we were driving home from Granny's house.
It started snowing. After an hour the snow was
really heavy. Dad couldn't see where he was going.
The car started sliding on the road. Sally was scared
and so was I. Suddenly the car skidded off the road
and crashed into a tree. It sounded like an explosion.
Mum screamed. Luckily none of us was hurt.

After that we got out of the car to see what
had happened to it. The front was dented and
the engine would not start.

Next we walked down the road to find
a phone. I was so cold that my feet felt like
blocks of ice. The snow blew in my eyes,
so I could hardly see a thing. No cars came
by and we didn't see a single phone.

Finally we came to a house. We ran to the door
and knocked as hard as we could. The lady who lived
there let us use her phone to call a breakdown truck.
She said we looked like a family of snowmen!
She gave us some hot chocolate while we waited.

Mum and Dad said we had both been really brave
about the crash and the snowy walk.

Writing a recount

Choose a set of pictures and write an action-packed recount.

1. Decide who to be.
2. Look at the pictures. Work out what happens and how it ends.
3. Think of a title.
4. Write about the pictures in order. Start a new paragraph for each picture.
5. End by making a comment about what happened.

3

4

When you write a recount:

- use words like after, later and next to give your reader an idea of when things happened.

- describe your feelings at each stage to make your recount even more interesting.

A DREAM JOB

Imagine you have stepped back in time. You see this advert. What sort of letter would you write to persuade Captain Scott to take you with him?

Ed Venture made a list of his skills and talents.

Determined and brave

Excellent cook

Strong swimmer

Fit and healthy

Champion skier

Keen camper

Animal expert

Experienced fisherman

Skilled navigator

Ed Venture used his list to write a persuasive letter to Captain Scott.

I hope he chooses me!

He included as many reasons as possible to show why he was the best person for the job.

Address in the top right-hand corner

ins with ar...'

things n do

asive uage

s with

s his e

Hill Farm
Kelso
Scotland
25th January 1909

Date under address

Dear Captain Scott,

I see from your advert that you are looking for exceptional people to travel with you to the South Pole.

I am 24 years old and very fit and healthy. I am an experienced fisherman and love being at sea. I am a very strong swimmer. While on the night watch I taught myself to navigate, using the stars. I am also an excellent cook.

I am sure it would be useful to have someone on your expedition who can look after animals. I am used to caring for animals and know cures for many common illnesses. I therefore think I would be a great help to you.

I have always dreamed of exploring unknown places, especially snowy ones, as I love to camp and ski.

Yours sincerely,

Ed Venture

This Ed Venture sounds just right for the job!

Applying for a job

Which of these two jobs would you prefer?

Can you think of reasons why you should be chosen? Don't be shy – sing your own praises!

WANTED!
Brave pilot
to be a navigator
on
an exciting
round-the-world flight.

Apply in writing to: Ms Amelia Earhart

Write a letter to one of these people from the past. Try to persuade them that you are the right person for the job.

1 First think of all the reasons why you would suit the job.

2 Write your address and the date in the right hand corner.

3 Start the letter with 'Dear...'.

WANTED!

Actors

able to

sing, dance and perform
in the plays of
Mr William Shakespeare

at a

London Theatre

Apply in writing to: Mr Richard Burbage

WRITING TIPS

4 Say who you are and write a bit about each of your good points.

5 Finish with 'Yours sincerely'.

6 Sign your full name.

When you write your letter:

- use persuasive language to convince the person that you are ideal for the job.

- only list skills that are useful for the job.